Practical Phrenology

Theodore Foster

Alpha Editions

This edition published in 2024

ISBN 9789361472992

Design and Setting By

Alpha Editions

www.alphaedis.com

Email - info@alphaedis.com

As per information held with us this book is in Public Domain.
This book is a reproduction of an important historical work.
Alpha Editions uses the best technology to reproduce historical work
in the same manner it was first published to preserve its original nature.
Any marks or number seen are left intentionally to preserve.

Contents

PREFACE.	- 1 -
DOMESTIC PROPENSITIES.	- 2 -
1. AMATIVENESS.	- 2 -
2. PHILOPROGENITIVENESS.	- 3 -
3. ADHESIVENESS.	- 4 -
4. INHABITIVENESS.	- 5 -
5. CONCENTRATIVENESS.	- 6 -
SELFISH PROPENSITIES.	- 7 -
1. COMBATIVENESS.	- 7 -
2. DESTRUCTIVENESS.	- 8 -
3. SECRETIVENESS.	- 9 -
4. ACQUISITIVENESS.	- 10 -
5. ALIMENTIVENESS.	- 12 -
SELFISH SENTIMENTS.	- 13 -
1. FIRMNESS.	- 13 -
2. SELF-ESTEEM.	- 14 -
3. LOVE OF APPROBATION.	- 16 -
4. CAUTIOUSNESS.	- 17 -
MORAL SENTIMENTS.	- 19 -
1. CONSCIENTIOUSNESS.	- 19 -
2. VENERATION.	- 20 -
3. BENEVOLENCE.	- 21 -
4. HOPE.	- 22 -
5. MARVELLOUSNESS.	- 23 -
INTELLECTUAL SENTIMENTS.	- 25 -

1. IDEALITY.	- 25 -
2. CONSTRUCTIVENESS.	- 26 -
3. IMITATION.	- 26 -
4. MIRTHFULNESS.	- 27 -
OBSERVING FACULTIES.	- 29 -
1. INDIVIDUALITY.	- 29 -
2. FORM.	- 30 -
3. SIZE.	- 30 -
4. WEIGHT.	- 31 -
5. COLOUR.	- 31 -
6. ORDER.	- 32 -
7. CALCULATION.	- 33 -
8. LOCALITY.	- 34 -
9. EVENTUALITY.	- 35 -
10. TIME.	- 35 -
11. TUNE.	- 36 -
12. LANGUAGE.	- 36 -
REFLECTIVE FACULTIES.	- 38 -
1. CAUSALITY.	- 38 -
2. COMPARISON.	- 39 -
TEMPERAMENTS.	- 41 -
THE END.	- 41 -

PREFACE.

THE present volume is designed to exhibit the subject of Practical Phrenology in as clear and as perspicuous a light as its nature will admit. To this purpose the author has aimed to divest it of all extraneous matter, and at the same time to avoid all unnecessary conciseness. The learner will here find a comprehensive view of the functions of each organ, with their different effects on the character when in various stages of developement, and also when compounded with each other.

The author presents few claims to originality. In a few instances he has even adopted the language of others where it presented itself in a felicitous manner—his aim being to make a good book rather than to add to his own reputation.

It is but proper here to state that the work has passed through the press without the benefit of the author's personal inspection—an affection of the eyes rendering this service impossible. But for this it might have received many *retouches*, which, if they did not add materially to its *value*, might have improved its appearance.

DOMESTIC PROPENSITIES.

1. AMATIVENESS.

THIS organ produces the sexual passion, and imparts to its possessor a desire for the happiness of the opposite sex. In society it does much to promote general kindliness of feeling, and urbanity of manners.

PREDOMINANT.—One in whom this organ predominates, will incline to be libidinous, licentious and lustful. If his moral organs are very large, particularly Firmness and Conscientiousness, he may restrain the outward expression of this feeling; but it will, nevertheless, be powerful, and at times overwhelming. If long deprived of the society of the other sex, he will feel lonesome and disconsolate.

LARGE.—With large Amativeness and Adhesiveness, an individual will be exceedingly attached to the society of the other sex; and will be capable of readily ingratiating himself into their favour. If with these organs large, and small Firmness and Conscientiousness, although his love will be intense and fervid, yet he will be apt to be capricious and fickle in his attachments. He will be inclined rather to seek the favour of the sex generally, than to limit his regard to a single object. If Adhesiveness, Inhabitiveness and Philoprogenitiveness are large, he will be induced to marry early, but if Adhesiveness, Philoprogenitiveness, and Conscientiousness are small, he will be inclined to gratify this feeling without reference to the laws of morality. With Self-esteem, Firmness, and Secretiveness large, although he may love intensely, yet he will not allow his passion to predominate over him; if disappointed, he will not be subdued, but manifest to the spectator the appearance of unconcern. With such a combination, he will, in all cases, feel much more intensely than his expressions will imply. If Mirthfulness is large, and Conscientiousness and Ideality small, he will be liable to joke, and be fond of licentious allusions.

MODERATE.—With a moderate developement of this organ, an individual will take great pleasure in the society of ladies, whose taste and feelings coincide with his own. If his Moral Sentiments and Intellect are large, he will be averse to the society of the merely volatile and frivolous. If Ideality and Love of Approbation are large, he will be attracted by the company of the gay and fashionable. If Ideality and Intellect generally, are large, he will be disgusted with vulgarity and libidinous allusions. His passion will be deep, but not lasting, and with a moderate amount of controlling organs he can restrain it at will.

SMALL.—When this organ is small, an individual will be distant and reserved towards females. If Adhesiveness is large, he may be attached to the society of a select few; but the connexion will be of a strictly Platonic character. He will be unable to feel the peculiar pleasures of female society. If Adhesiveness and Philoprogenitiveness are large, he may be disposed to a matrimonial alliance; but if these organs are small, he will be decidedly averse to such a connexion. If one with Moral Sentiments moderate, and Destructiveness and Self-esteem large, under the influence of the aforementioned combination, were to marry, the connexion would be necessarily an unfortunate one; his attachment could not outlive the vicissitudes attending the marriage state, and would inevitably degenerate into disdain and aversion. He would, notwithstanding, be a fond parent, though his affection would be capricious and ill regulated. With Adhesiveness, Conscientiousness, Veneration, and Benevolence large, an individual's regard for the wife of his choice, if fortunate in his selection, will increase with time; the strength of his superior sentiments more than supplying the want of animal passion.

2. PHILOPROGENITIVENESS.

THE legitimate office of this organ is to produce love for one's own offspring. It produces, however, in the breast of its possessor an affection for children indiscriminately; for the feeble and helpless; for pets—as dogs, horses, cats, &c., and even for inanimate objects. It has an influence in producing general kindliness of disposition. A peculiarity of its character consists in its inspiring its possessor to love with the fondest affection the child that is the most helpless, and even the one that has caused the greatest solicitude and brought down on its parent the deepest disgrace.

PREDOMINANT.—An individual in whom this organ predominates has a constant hankering for the society of children. If without them himself, he views the deprivation as a great misfortune, and if his circumstances are favourable, will be likely to adopt one, for the purpose of exhausting the energy of this feeling upon it. He will be likewise much attached to pets, as horses and dogs.

LARGE.—Those who possess this organ large, betray it in every look and motion when in company with children. They take the greatest delight in their society, and enter into their little troubles and enjoyments with the greatest zeal. They readily enlist their confidence, and can easily control them. If deprived of their society, they will exhaust their attachment upon some pet animal which they will frequently fondle. When Combativeness, Destructiveness and Philoprogenitiveness are large, an individual will punish children severely when they annoy him, notwithstanding his great affection for them. If Self-esteem and Combativeness are small, he will be liable to humour his children and allow them improper indulgences. With Combativeness and Destructiveness large, he will be apt to be capricious in his feelings towards children, at one time humoring them, and at another petulant and cross.

MODERATE.—With Philoprogenitiveness moderate, a person will be attached to his own children to a good degree, and may take some interest in others after they begin to lose their infantile character. This feeling, however, will not be durable. He will readily tire of children when they annoy him. The death of a child will be a poignant affliction to him, but it will be soon forgotten. If Destructiveness and Self-esteem are large, he will be liable to punish them with severity for trivial offences.

SMALL.—With this organ small, a person will be exceedingly annoyed by children. If a parent, he will consign the care of them to menials. In all his intercourse with company, he will betray a marked indifference to their society. If ever induced to amuse them, his awkwardness will betray itself to the most casual observer. If Benevolence is large, he will take all needful care of them; but if Secretiveness and Destructiveness are large, he will delight to torment and teaze them.

3. ADHESIVENESS.

THIS organ furnishes the instinct of social attachment. Towards the object of its regard it excites the purest feelings of affection. It is not satisfied with loving, it must also be loved, and requires for its healthy existence a constant exchange of pure and radiant affection. It diffuses its influence over the whole character of the man, and tends to render him kind, amiable, and affectionate. It leads to the love of company, and of social intercourse. While it is the germ of many virtues, it is to be feared; in the present state of society, it is likewise productive of many vices.

PREDOMINANT.—With Adhesiveness predominant, an individual is pre-eminently qualified to enjoy friendship, and will be miserable without it. He will often feel the yearnings of affection coming over him with all the intensity of a passion. His most vivid enjoyments are experienced in the society of his friends. He readily recognises the existence of a similar feeling in another, and, if circumstances are favourable, they soon become intimate.

LARGE.—One having Adhesiveness large, is eminently social and affectionate. With large Moral organs, will make great sacrifices to render his friends service, and will esteem the pleasures of friendship as one of the chief sources of enjoyment. With Combativeness and Destructiveness large, and Self-esteem moderate, will resent an aggression upon a friend which he would not notice upon himself. If Self-esteem is large, with Combativeness and Destructiveness large, he will easily get angry with his friends, but will be readily conciliated. With Benevolence and Love of Approbation large, is exceedingly liberal and forward among friends; will do his utmost to please and gratify them; earnestly desire their approbation; and will be exceedingly sensitive to their reproaches. With Firmness and Conscientiousness small, will be capricious in his attachments. With Secretiveness and Self-esteem large, he will not fully express the feelings which he experiences, and will thus leave the impression that his affection is less than it really is.

MODERATE.—One having Adhesiveness moderate, may be strongly attached to friends, but his friendships will be readily severed. He may be companionable, and with large Benevolence will be generous and good-hearted, but he will still lack that strong feeling of sympathy without which friendship is but a name.

SMALL.—With Adhesiveness small, an individual will be unsocial, cold-hearted and selfish. If his moral organs predominate over self-esteem, he may be companionable, but he will be nearly wanting in the attributes of character ascribed to this organ.

4. INHABITIVENESS.

THIS organ produces home-sickness, and causes a feeling of regret to take possession of the mind when leaving a place in which one has long resided. It is the first element of patriotism. It produces a desire to locate and reside in a particular place, and adds much to the strength of family attachments.

PREDOMINANT.—One in whom Inhabitiveness predominates, is pre-eminently attached to any place with which he has become familiar. It causes him much pain to leave it, and he returns to it with eagerness.

LARGE.—One having inhabitiveness large, will experience the most poignant sensations of regret at leaving a place with which he has become familiar. Even a particular house, garden, office or room, has for him peculiar gratifications. With large Locality, will take delight in travelling, but will be constantly harassed by thoughts of home. This is more especially the case if Concentrativeness is large. If Self-esteem and Veneration are large, he will be eminently patriotic, and will defend his country from aspersions with as much vigour as himself. Veneration being large, he will experience the profoundest feelings of respect and regard for the memory of the departed worthies of its history; and with large Individuality, Eventuality, &c., he will take great delight in reading the history of his own country, and of conversing upon its character and institutions. If long absent from home, he is constantly curious, and eagerly seeks every means of being informed concerning it. The peculiarities of the different places in which he has resided often occur to him with feelings of the most vivid pleasure.

MODERATE.—One in whom Inhabitiveness is moderate, will not change his residence without regret, yet soon becomes reconciled to a new location. If long absent from his country, Self-esteem being small, he will become expatriated in feeling, and identify himself wholly with the country in which he resides.

SMALL.—When Inhabitiveness is small, the individual will be constantly prompted to change his place of residence. Unless this feeling is counteracted by the strength of other organs, he cannot get familiarized with a place without becoming dissatisfied and restless.

5. CONCENTRATIVENESS.

THIS organ imparts the power of continuity of thought. It also aids in enabling its possessor to continue the action of the organs generally.

PREDOMINANT.—One having Concentrativeness predominant, with Causality large, will be much subject to absence of mind. He will be quite unable to attend to more than one thing at a time, and will be generally prolix in conversation.

LARGE.—With large Concentrativeness, an individual will be much disturbed if more than one thing claim attention at once; has a strong inclination after taking up a subject to pursue it till he has completed it. In conversation he will be much distracted if it is desultory in its character. If a writer, his compositions will exhibit a sustained unity of expression throughout.

MODERATE.—One with Concentrativeness moderate, is inclined to pursue a subject or train of thought, but can be easily diverted from it. If Causality and Intellect generally are moderate, is neither inclined to pursue a study to its termination, nor is he able to pass rapidly to another. With nervous temperament he will possess great versatility of attention.

SMALL.—With Concentrativeness small, an individual will be quite unable to devote his attention for any length of time to a single study or subject. In ordinary conversation, he will fly from one subject to another, without order or arrangement. His friends, even if strongly attached to them, will not be long thought of at a time. His antipathies will be readily assuaged. He will possess great vivacity of disposition.

SELFISH PROPENSITIES.

1. COMBATIVENESS.

THIS organ gives the desire to oppose, resist and overcome. It renders its possessor able to encounter difficulties, and to be bold and strenuous in his opposition. If not properly regulated, it leads to a desire to contradict and quarrel for the sake of opposition. It gives vigour and zeal to the pugilist and warrior.

PREDOMINANT.—When this organ predominates, the individual will be bold, disputatious and quarrelsome. In an encounter he will never be satisfied till he has obtained the mastery. He will display great nerve and determination in whatever he undertakes. With Self-esteem large, and Conscientiousness and Benevolence small, he will be extremely quarrelsome and overbearing.

LARGE.—With Self-esteem large, the individual will be pre-eminently bold and enterprising. If Firmness is small, he will be wavering in his views; but if Firmness is large, he will add perseverance to courage, and never give up a point while a reasonable hope of success remains. If with this combination, and Moral Sentiments small, he will be litigious and quarrelsome. If Destructiveness is small, he will be fond of disputing, but will avoid giving pain. If Destructiveness is large, and Benevolence small, he will be vindictive and cruel, and will ever be disposed to vindicate his own importance, regardless of circumstances or the rights of others. If Love of Approbation, Benevolence, Veneration and Conscientiousness are large, he will avoid all low contentions, and will direct the action of this organ to the maintenance of right and the enforcement of just opinion.

MODERATE.—One with moderate Combativeness, will forbear in a contention as long as Self-esteem will allow. If his temperament is active, he may be irritable and passionate, but upon the whole, will be peaceable. If his religious feelings are strong, notwithstanding his usual distaste for opposition, he will contend strenuously for the rights of his church, and cheerfully encounter reproach for its sake. If Acquisitiveness is large, and Self-esteem small, he will allow himself to be insulted with impunity, but will resist every attack upon his property.

SMALL.—With Combativeness small, an individual's character will be mild and peaceable. He will rather submit to oppression than make the requisite exertion to defend his rights. Above every thing else he will desire peace. With Self-esteem small, he will be eminently deficient in presence of mind in times of danger. He will quail under opposition, and with Cautiousness large, will be timid and cowardly. With Destructiveness large, and Benevolence small, he will be harsh and severe where there is no resentment to be feared. With Acquisitiveness large, he will be fond of acquiring by slow accumulations, rather than by bold speculations. With Domestic Feelings large, he will avoid the turbulent scenes of life, and seek refuge in quiet and retirement.

2. DESTRUCTIVENESS.

THIS organ produces the propensity to exterminate and destroy. It incites the murderer to his act of crime. It renders its possessor harsh, cruel, and indifferent to the feelings of others, and is an active element in the minds of all warriors, sportsmen and pugilists.

PREDOMINANT.—With Destructiveness predominant, an individual will be harsh, cruel and severe. His language will abound with pungent sarcasms and cutting remarks. With large Combativeness, he will prefer arms as a profession. With Self-esteem and Combativeness both large, he will be distinguished for his energy and force of character. He will drive through his purposes regardless of opposition.

LARGE.—With Destructiveness large, and Benevolence small, an individual will be cruel, sanguinary and severe. With Secretiveness and Conscientiousness small, and Combativeness and Self-esteem large, he will be exceedingly passionate and vindictive. With such a combination, he will lose no opportunity of assailing the feelings of his opponents. If Amativeness and Adhesiveness are large, he will be attached to his family, yet will treat them often with great severity. If Combativeness and Destructiveness are small, it will require much to excite him, but when aroused, he will be vindictive to the last degree. If Benevolence is large, he will not be sanguinary or cruel; but with Combativeness moderate, will be mild and amiable in disposition, yet capable of great severity when circumstances justify it. This combination enables the surgeon to perform an operation with the requisite energy, and yet without giving unnecessary pain. With Approbativeness small, and Self-esteem, Conscientiousness and Benevolence large, he may be charitable, yet he will often give needless offence in his administrations of charity. He will destroy every thing that is not absolutely valuable.

MODERATE.—With Destructiveness moderate, and Benevolence large, one will be tender-hearted, and with small Combativeness, effeminate. With moderate Benevolence, and large Self-esteem and Combativeness, he will possess sufficient severity of character to enable him to succeed in any lawful occupation. He will be naturally peaceful and opposed to harsh measures when they can be avoided, yet will not refrain from using severity when necessary. If Benevolence is large, and Combativeness and Self-esteem moderate, he will lack energy and force of mind; will easily sink under difficulties and submit quietly to aggression and imposition.

SMALL.—With Destructiveness small, an individual will be effeminate, and with moderate Combativeness, be very destitute of energy and force of character. He will be mild, inoffensive, and peaceable. The performance of an action that requires the infliction of much pain, will be to him nearly impossible. With Acquisitiveness moderate or large, he will have a desire to preserve and lay by every thing that is not absolutely worthless. It will give him pain to see any thing that may possibly be of service destroyed.

3. SECRETIVENESS.

THIS organ gives the desire and the talents for concealment. In its abuse, it renders its possessor averse to, and almost incapable of, an open-hearted expression. His remarks are sly, evasive and ambiguous. His actions, he considers, are beyond the reach of human sagacity. It is the foundation of all hypocrisy, deception and intrigue.

PREDOMINANT.—One in whom Secretiveness predominates, will be sly, conniving and hypocritical. It will be difficult for him to relate the simplest incident without evasion. If he has an end to bring about, he will seek to do it by some manœuvre, even when an open course would be more effective. The most trifling actions of his life will be brought about by stratagem. He looks upon others as being actuated by the same motives as himself, and is constantly suspicious and watchful. He will possess great tact, and be readily enabled to discover the motives of others. In conversation, he is apt to hesitate and recommence his sentences, and to answer in an ambiguous manner.

LARGE.—With Secretiveness, Self-esteem and Conscientiousness large, an individual will detest hypocrisy and duplicity, yet will be exceedingly prudent and circumspect in his conversation and conduct. He will be slow to make acquaintances, and will require a long time ere he becomes intimate with them. With Love of Approbation large, he will be deferential and polite, and will possess a superior tact at making himself agreeable. With Comparison and Individuality large, he will possess a good knowledge of human nature, will be well qualified to detect intrigue, and of frustrating any designs upon himself. If Self-esteem, Firmness and Secretiveness are large, he will endure pain with the most heroic fortitude and forbearance. If Conscientiousness be moderate, he will be very suspicious towards others, and will be perpetually on his guard. If Destructiveness and Self-esteem are large, he will be easily made angry, but with Cautiousness and Firmness large, will restrain his feelings even when highly excited. With Conscientiousness and Cautiousness large, it will be exceedingly difficult for him to form an opinion. With Adhesiveness moderate, and Imitation large, he will be liable to be very friendly to one's face, and abuse him in his absence. With Self-esteem and Firmness large, will seldom yield to an opponent, but will very often deceive him by appearing to have yielded.

MODERATE.—With Secretiveness moderate, and Self-esteem large, one will be frank, candid and open-hearted in his ordinary intercourse with society, yet will be capable, when necessity requires it, of intrigue and duplicity. He will be frank, open and sincere to acquaintances, yet will manifest much reserve to strangers. His ordinary conversation will be discreet, yet, when excited, he will express his sentiments regardless of consequences; this is more particularly true when Cautiousness is small. He will then be distinguished for contrariety of feeling, being prudent and circumspect at one time, and open, blunt and offending at another. Conscientiousness being small, adds much to the strength of Secretiveness. He will then use deception and intrigue whenever they answer his purpose. If Self-esteem, Combativeness and Destructiveness are large, he will be very blunt and decided, when nothing is to be gained by an opposite course, and will express his sentiments without scruple.

SMALL.—With Secretiveness small, one is frank, candid and open-hearted. He will freely relate even to comparative strangers all his foibles and weaknesses, as well as his virtues and merits. He expresses his hatred and dislikes without fear or favour. Strangers will suppose his anger or displeasure to be greater than it really is. With Destructiveness and Self-esteem large, he will get angry readily, but if Concentrativeness is small, will soon recover his temper. He will be often imposed upon in consequence of his relying too much on others. If Love of Approbation and Benevolence are small, his demeanour will be usually gruff and impolite. He will have great aversion to outside show, will use plain and blunt expressions, and be fond of forcible language.

4. ACQUISITIVENESS.

THIS organ produces the desire to save, to hoard up and accumulate. It induces its possessor to acquire property without reference to its uses or his own necessities. It produces the instinct of property.

PREDOMINANT.—A person in whom this organ predominates, will be miserly, sordid and avaricious. He will look upon the accumulation of property as the great end of human existence. If with a low education, he will not scruple to steal and pilfer.

LARGE.—With large Acquisitiveness, and small Benevolence, an individual will be selfish, sordid and grasping; but with large Conscientiousness, he will not trespass on the rights of others. With Domestic Feelings small, he will be excessively penurious in regard to his family, and will begrudge every shilling that is expended for their benefit; but if Domestic Feelings are large, he will spend money freely for the comfort of his family, when he would not on his own account. With Love of Approbation and Ideality large, he will spend money freely, in order that he may excel in dress, equipage, &c., while at the same time, he will be excessively penurious in his dealings. With large Veneration, he will look with much respect and awe upon those who are distinguished for their wealth. With Love of Approbation large, he will be anxious to avoid the reputation of littleness in his dealings, and will often give to charitable objects, but will give in such a way as it shall be known. With Firmness, Self-esteem, Hope and Combativeness large, he will be eminently enterprising and persevering. If Caution is small, will be apt to rush into speculations heedlessly and recklessly; but if Caution is large, will be exceedingly prudent and careful in what he undertakes; but when he has come to a conclusion upon a point, he will pursue it with great zeal and energy. If Secretiveness is large, he will have great ability to make a bargain and effect an arrangement where many others would fail. If Cautiousness is large, and Hope and Self-esteem moderate or small, he will be averse to speculations and great enterprises, and prefer slow processes of accumulation. If Firmness is small, he will be apt to be fickle in his undertakings and not pursue them long enough to obtain his ends. If Conscientiousness and Veneration be large, he may be induced to give money to religious purposes. If Ideality and Veneration are large, he will be likely to hoard antiquities, medals, &c. With large Intellect, he will take great pleasure in accumulating a library. If Ideality and Love of Approbation are small, he will care little for the beauty of the binding or the neatness of the type; but with Ideality large, he will spend money freely for these luxuries. With Perceptive organs large, will be a good judge of property, &c.

MODERATE.—With moderate Acquisitiveness, Self-esteem and Love of Approbation, a person may be close and economical in his dealings, be shrewd, enterprising and industrious, may make and accumulate money, but he will often spend it unnecessarily. With every desire, as he supposes, to save, yet he will find at the end of the year that he has expended much that he might have saved. If Alimentiveness is large, he will be unable to deny himself the pleasures of the table. If Adhesiveness is large, he will spend money freely for the gratification of his friends. If Benevolence is large, he will give much to objects of charity. He will look upon money as the means of enjoyment, and not as the end of human exertion.

SMALL.—A person in whom Acquisitiveness is small, will be unable to understand the value of money, or to take pleasure in its acquisition, and unless restrained by the influence of the moral feelings, will be a spendthrift.

5. ALIMENTIVENESS.

THIS organ imparts the relish for food and drink. Its activity is increased when the person is engaged in eating or drinking.

PREDOMINANT.—One in whom this organ is predominant, will be greatly addicted to the pleasures of the table, will eat voraciously, and will consider gustatory enjoyments one of the chief pleasures of existence.

LARGE.—With Adhesiveness and Love of Approbation large, he will be very fond of public dinners and festive occasions. If to these be added Ideality large, the pleasures of these occasions will be heightened in proportion to the splendour of their appearance. If Acquisitiveness is large, there will be a continued struggle in his mind; the one wishing to save money and the other to indulge in good living: the contest will be decided by the character of his other developements and his worldly circumstances. If Acquisitiveness is small, he will be regardless of the expense of an entertainment, and will gratify his appetite without reference to its cost. With Adhesiveness, Ideality and Approbativeness large, he will take delight in entertaining his friends in a sumptuous manner. With Conscientiousness, Veneration and Benevolence large, he will often reproach himself for his extravagance in matters of the table. With Mirthfulness, Imitation and Secretiveness large, will be excessively fond of telling stories, and in "setting the table in a roar." With Ideality and Love of Approbation moderate, and Causality and Self-esteem large, will be fond of entertaining company, but will despise ceremony.

MODERATE.—With Alimentiveness moderate, a person is fond of a good diet, but does not make it a prominent object of his attention. With Benevolence large, he will cheerfully put up with meaner fare than he is accustomed to when necessity requires it. If Acquisitiveness is large, he will not expend much upon the pleasures of the palate.

SMALL.—With Alimentiveness small, an individual will be quite regardless of what he eats; will be unable to remember from one day to another what he has eaten, and usually finds it difficult to decide at table what dish to take first. With Destructiveness large, often speaks bitterly of those who indulge in luxurious living. With large Love of Approbation and Ideality, will give entertainments, but think more of the respectability of his company and the splendour of the appearance of his table, than of the quality of the food, &c.

SELFISH SENTIMENTS.

1. FIRMNESS.

THE tendency of this organ is to give constancy and perseverance to the other powers, and aids their activity and force. Its impulses are sometimes mistaken for will. This, however, is not correct, as the action of this organ urges *only to a continuance* in the same purpose, the same mode of thinking, and the same cause of action. It adds force to resolution, and is the active element in fortitude, perseverance and endurance. With a strong endowment of this organ, persons find it difficult to enter readily into the feelings of others, or to feel new emotions suddenly.

PREDOMINANT.—With Firmness predominant, a person will exhibit unyielding pertinacity of character throughout all the vicissitudes of life. No misfortune will appal him. His fortitude of character will enable him to rise superior to every affliction. Having once commenced a pursuit, he will never relinquish it till compelled to do so by the force of circumstances. His opinions will seldom change, and his whole appearance and manner will exhibit the man of firmness and decision. He may be a good master, but he will be an unwilling servant.

LARGE.—With this organ large, a person will be of an unmovable character, firm in his resolutions, and constant in his principles. He attends little to exhortations or examples, his conduct is uniform, and his exertions may be calculated on in all the various situations of life. With Combativeness and Self-esteem large, he will never relinquish a pursuit while a hope of success remains, and with but moderate Cautiousness and Causality, will be deaf to all remonstrance or advice. With large Benevolence and Conscientiousness, he will seek for independence, yet be just and benevolent. An attack upon his opinions will increase the tenacity with which he maintains them. With large Self-esteem, he will be distinguished for presence of mind in times of danger.

MODERATE.—With Firmness moderate, a person will continue constant only in those purposes in which he is aided by the other organs. If Conscientiousness is large, and the Selfish Propensities small, he will continue inflexibly just through all temptations of life. If Acquisitiveness is large, he will never waver in his pursuit of riches. If Self-esteem is small, and Love of Approbation large, he will be entirely dependent on the will of his associates. It will be quite impossible for him to have an opinion of his own.

SMALL.—With Firmness small, a person cannot be said to have a will of his own. He will follow the last impulse he receives, and without strength to resist, will be an easy instrument of every one he meets. The actions of his life will take their character from the other organs, and he will thus be constant in the gratification of predominant dispositions. With large Acquisitiveness, he will be constant in his efforts to become rich, but he will be unsteady in the means he employs. With large Benevolence, Combativeness and Destructiveness, he will be now all kindness, and anon passionate, violent and outrageous. With an active temperament, he will enter on his pursuits with great avidity, and follow them up with commendable zeal, until perhaps, near their accomplishment, and then fly away to something else. This state of mind is increased by great Cautiousness, and diminished by large Self-esteem.

2. SELF-ESTEEM.

THIS organ produces the feeling of individual personality, or of personal identity. It causes the feelings of self-love, self-respect, self-complacency. It imparts to the individual a high opinion of himself, and of every thing pertaining or belonging to himself. The most insignificant object, when in the possession of an individual with this feeling strong, assumes a value and an importance, in his own estimation, which nothing could have given it before. To such a person, the idea of self is perpetually before him. Let an idea be suggested, and his first consideration will be as to how it will affect his own condition. It gives a cold and repulsive appearance to the individual, and renders him particularly obnoxious to others having the same organization. It renders one averse to submission, and gives an inclination to assume the lead. When properly regulated, it adds dignity to the whole demeanour, and gives a nobleness to the character which effectually prevents any action of meanness or servility.

PREDOMINANT.—With this organ predominant, an individual will be proud, haughty and supercilious. Whatever he possesses, he considers superior to that belonging to any one else. In his judgment and actions he scorns all advice, and looks down with contempt on his fellow-men. He admits no dictation. He never submits to advice, but assumes the lead on all occasions. Any thing like familiarity revolts him. His whole appearance indicates assurance and presumption. When excited, he is disposed to go to the greatest extremes. "He will have many enemies, and will be regardless of the frown or the favour of men; intractable, domineering, repulsive, conceited, jealous, austere, he considers himself nearly infallible."

LARGE.—With this organ large, the individual is endowed with that degree of self-complacency which enables him to apply his powers to the best advantage, in every situation in which he may be placed. With

Combativeness and Firmness large, and Destructiveness moderate, he is eminently qualified to sustain himself in any situation in which he may be placed. With this organization, he will be bold, energetic, persevering, and surpassingly independent. No difficulties will appal him, and no force of circumstances of an ordinary character, will deter him from the prosecution of his designs. With large Conscientiousness, he will be honourable and high-minded in the extreme. With large Conscientiousness, Veneration, Ideality, Benevolence and Causality, he will rather suffer death than commit a dishonourable action. If Conscientiousness, Benevolence and Veneration are deficient, he will be dogmatic, imperious and haughty, and will be constantly striving for power, which, when obtained, he invariably abuses. If an author, with Ideality, Language and Comparison large, he will write in a sustained and lofty style, never descending to a common-place expression. If his Domestic Feelings are large, with Combativeness and Destructiveness large, he will be tenderly attached to his family, and take great pride and interest in them, yet will require from them implicit obedience. With Cautiousness and Causality large, he will be induced to seek advice, but only for the purpose of enabling him to form his own opinion. With Cautiousness large, he will often appear disconcerted and diffident, in consequence of his anxiety about matters likely to affect him. With Firmness, Secretiveness and Imitation large, a person will never act in a subordinate station. Let his situation in life be what it may, he will always be a leader.

MODERATE.—With Self-esteem moderate, and with a favourable developement of other organs, one will have sufficient self-respect for the ordinary occupations of life, but he will never be able to put himself forward in any great undertaking, or to command that general influence and esteem as he would do with a larger developement of this organ. With Cautiousness, Love of Approbation and Veneration large, he will be humble, timid and abashed in the presence of superiors or strangers. He will lack the requisite independence to vindicate his own opinion, and will be too ready to give way to that of others. With this organization, and large Intellect, he may possess great abilities, but for want of self-confidence requisite to enable him to make his way through opposition, he will be much underrated. It will give him pain to be obliged to trespass on the attention of others, and he will suffer greatly from a feeling of unworthiness. With small Cautiousness, Firmness, Combativeness and Destructiveness, he will be enterprising and persevering, yet will lack that force of character requisite for important undertakings. With large Veneration, Conscientiousness and Intellect, he will be respectful towards others, and will not be deficient in respect for himself.

SMALL.—With Self-esteem small, one will be humble and submissive. No matter how exalted may be the character of his intellect, a feeling of unworthiness will accompany all his actions. He will ever associate with inferiors. His language will be trifling and common-place. Let his talents be what they may, he will never rise from an inferior station.

3. LOVE OF APPROBATION.

THIS organ excites the desire of notice, praise, distinction and recognition. It is an active element in the mind of the office seeker, the soldier, the actor, the statesman, &c. It inspires the fop, and sustains the buffoon. It causes a desire to be approved as well as noticed, but it prefers censure to inattention. When properly regulated, it induces amiability of disposition.

PREDOMINANT.—An individual with this organ predominant, will be grossly vain and fantastical. Every action of his life will be calculated to excite attention. He will appear to think as though the world had little else to do than to be attentive to his actions.

LARGE.—With this organ large, a person will be distinguished for the regard he places upon his character. The disapprobation of his fellow-men will be displeasing to him in a high degree. In his intercourse with society, he will be polite and courteous, avoiding every thing harsh, austere or repulsive. If Conscientiousness and Intellect are deficient, he will be a braggart, and will often speak of his feats and performances. If thrown into evil company, he will be foremost in all deeds of wickedness. With Self-esteem large, and Causality moderate or small, will be exceedingly proud and vain, will use much ceremony, and will be very affected in his manner and conversation; and if Ideality and Individuality are large, will be exceedingly fond of dress and finical decorations. With Adhesiveness large, and Firmness moderate or small, one will be influenced by the opinions of his friends and associates, and will give way to them in opposition to the dictates of his own judgment. With this combination, and Destructiveness and Combativeness large, will get easily offended, and construe the least inattention from his friends into dislike or insult. With Cautiousness, Secretiveness, Veneration and Conscientiousness large, or very large, and Self-esteem small, will be very desirous to please, and will evince great anxiety to carry out this object; will feel great respect for superiors in age, talents, &c.; will entertain a feeling of his own inferiority, and also of reserve, which will have the effect of making him timid and bashful. With Combativeness, Destructiveness, Self-esteem, Firmness, Ideality, Individuality, Eventuality and Language large, and Comparison and Causality large, will possess talents for an exalted order, and an ardent ambition of fame. This combination will enable him to distinguish himself for intellectual greatness.

MODERATE.—With this organ but moderately developed, a person will by no means be insensible to the opinions of the world, yet, if Self-esteem and Conscientiousness are large, he will not allow its opinions to force him from the path of duty. If Adhesiveness is large, the opinion of his friends will have much influence over him. If Firmness, Self-esteem and Combativeness are large, he will be austere and independent, doing what his own feelings dictate, regardless of the frowns or favours of his fellow-men.

SMALL.—With Love of Approbation small, one will almost be insensible to the feelings of shame, and will be nearly regardless of public opinion. With small Ideality, he will be slovenly in his dress and appearance.

4. CAUTIOUSNESS.

THIS organ is the parent of fear. It urges its possessor to use every precaution possible for his individual safety. It is excited by every object that has power to affect his condition, or the condition of the objects of his other feelings. It renders one prudent, circumspect and judicious.

PREDOMINANT.—When this organ predominates, the individual will be timid, irresolute and undecided. He will never by any accident give way to a flow of ideas. For the most insignificant undertakings he will prepare with the greatest precaution, and will never form a connexion without subjecting it to the most rigorous examination. If Destructiveness is large, and Hope not more than moderate, he will be liable to commit suicide.

LARGE.—With Cautiousness large, a person will be habitually careful, cautious and prudent in all his transactions in life. He will never take a step without due consideration. If Self-esteem, Combativeness and Destructiveness are large, he will be wary and prudent in entering upon an undertaking, but when he has commenced, he will prosecute it with great energy and boldness.

MODERATE.—With but a moderate developement of this organ, and with large Hope and Self-esteem, one will be habitually reckless and imprudent; but if these organs are small, and Causality and Comparison large, he will not lack discretion in ordinary occupations of life, or in cases where his other organs create a lively interest. If Acquisitiveness is large, he will be prudent in business transactions. If the Domestic Feelings are strong, he will be anxious respecting the welfare of his family; and if Love of Approbation is strong, he will be particularly careful in whatever regards his own reputation.

SMALL.—With Cautiousness small, a person will act according to the dictates of his other faculties, unrestrained by timidity or fear. He will be rash, precipitate and perfectly regardless of the results of his conduct. If with a sanguine temperament, and Hope moderate or large, his disposition will be gay and cheerful, and will be too much engrossed with the present.

MORAL SENTIMENTS.

1. CONSCIENTIOUSNESS.

THIS organ views all actions in their moral aspect. It operates as an internal monitor, prescribing to its possessor the claims of truth and duty. Its power, however, does not enable it to decide upon what is abstractly just or unjust. This is affected by the character of the other organs with which it is combined. A person with large conscientiousness, and large Selfish Propensities, will consider an action just, which another, with the same amount of Conscientiousness, and smaller propensities, will consider unjust. This organ is essential to the formation of a truly philosophic mind, especially in moral investigations. It produces the desire of discovering the tact of recognising it when discovered, and that perfect reliance on its invincible supremacy which gives at once dignity and peace to the mind.

PREDOMINANT.—When this organ predominates, the individual looks always and only for truth, and receives it from whatever source it comes. He is thus disposed to regulate his conduct by the wisest sentiments of justice, which imparts an earnestness, integrity and directness in his manner, that leaves no room to doubt of his sincerity. He desires to act justly from the love of justice, unbiased by fear, interest or any sinister motive. When the actions have been contrary to the dictates of this organ, it produces remorse, repentance, a sense of guilt and demerit.

LARGE.—With this organ large, and the Selfish Propensities moderate, one will be eminently just and honest in all his dealings. He can never be brought to sacrifice duty to expediency. With large Firmness and Combativeness, he will be particularly firm, bold and decided on all questions of moral duty. He will never shrink from the advocacy of right, or from sustaining the defenceless from the unjust attacks of their enemies. If with this combination, Destructiveness is large, he will be inclined to severely censure any trickery or dishonesty in others; and if Causality is not large, he will consider himself the standard of truth and justice, by which all others must be judged.

MODERATE.—With but a moderate developement of this organ, one will endeavour to act justly; and if Causality and Comparison are large, and the Selfish Propensities small, he will generally do so; but if the Selfish Propensities are very strong, he will be guided more by considerations of interest than of duty. If with this combination, and Adhesiveness large, while he will take advantage of a stranger in a pecuniary transaction, no power of circumstances can induce him to trespass on the rights of a friend. His compunctions of conscience will be few and feeble. He will not be scrupulous about what he requires of others, seeming to claim as a right, that they should make sacrifices to his interest and inclination. He will look more to the effect that actions and opinions will have upon himself, than upon their moral character. If Love of Approbation, Secretiveness and Destructiveness are large, he will be likely to indulge in harsh, censorious and unjust remarks upon the character of his neighbours, while at the same time, if Acquisitiveness is moderate or small, he will be strictly just in all his dealings.

SMALL.—With Conscientiousness small, one will have few or no compunctions of conscience; he will be ever ready to justify himself to himself, have little or no regard for moral principle, and an imperfect idea of right and wrong in the abstract. With large Self-esteem, Benevolence, and Adhesiveness, and with small Acquisitiveness and Secretiveness, he may be honest and kind-hearted in his general conduct, but it will be because he considers it dishonourable and unmanly to commit a mean action, and because it pains his Benevolence and Adhesiveness to injure another. With this combination he will extol his friends in the highest terms, but if he gets angry with them, he will traduce and vilify them, being in both cases regardless of their true merit. If Love of Approbation is large, he will adopt every means to please without regard to justice or propriety.

2. VENERATION.

THIS organ produces the sentiment of reverence, without regarding the character of the object on which it seeks exercise. By its influence man adores God, venerates saints, and respects parents, teachers and superiors in general. This organ is the source of natural religion, or that tendency to worship a superior power which manifests itself in every nation yet discovered.

PREDOMINANT.—With Veneration predominant, a person if religious, will be extremely devout, and will experience the most profound feelings of awe and respect in contemplating the attributes of the deity. If Marvellousness and Conscientiousness are large, he will be extremely susceptible of religious impressions, and will not fail to become a devout and enthusiastic adherent of the church.

LARGE.—A person with Veneration large, will feel profound respect for all persons and objects that are aged and venerable, or in any way entitled in his estimation to respect and confidence. With large Benevolence and Conscientiousness, he will not only act justly and charitably, but his actions will be accompanied and sustained by a feeling of respect and reverence for the abstract principles of justice and charity, that cannot be conceived by those who have this organ small. With large Love of Approbation, and small Conscientiousness, he will be disposed to think highly of those who are in high stations, the rich, the powerful and the grand. If Combativeness and Destructiveness are large, and Acquisitiveness small, while he may look with contempt upon the merely wealthy, he will feel much respect for the memory and character of the brave and patriotic. With large Intellect, the action of this organ will be exerted towards the character and persons of literary men.

MODERATE.—With this organ but moderately developed, the sentiment of respect in general will have but a limited influence over the character of the individual. If Conscientiousness and Marvellousness are large, he will probably be religious, but he will not be so devout and enthusiastic in his devotions as many others with less real piety. If Love of Approbation is large, he will be exceedingly courteous and attentive, but his conduct will lack that deference and respect so necessary to conciliate esteem.

SMALL.—With Veneration but small, a person will be almost wholly destitute of the qualities ascribed to this organ. He may be religious, but the act of devotion will be a task to him, and he will be enabled to conceive those feelings of solemnity and awe, with which many are exercised. Children so constituted are disobedient and inattentive to their parents and teachers.

3. BENEVOLENCE.

THIS organ produces the desire of the happiness of others, and disposes to compassion and goodness of heart. It produces liberality of sentiment towards all mankind, and a disposition to love them and contribute to their pleasures. The benevolent man cannot feel happy, as long as famine, bodily suffering and mental misery are the bitter portion of his fellow creatures. He will never complain of the heartlessness or the ingratitude of others. He is so well aware of wishing well to others, that he does not doubt of their good will towards himself.

PREDOMINANT.—With this organ predominant, one may almost be said to be the victim of his kindness, good will and sympathy to others. In his zeal for the welfare of his fellow creatures, he seldom thinks of himself. In society, he restrains all his selfish inclinations, for fear of giving uneasiness to others. He will frequently meditate upon the miseries of mankind, and consider the various means of relieving their wretchedness.

LARGE.—With Benevolence large, one will be kind, charitable and forgiving. His whole demeanour will indicate goodness of disposition. If Secretiveness is small, he will be especially liable to imposition, as he will be conscious of entertaining no designs against others, and will suspect none against himself. If Adhesiveness is large, and Acquisitiveness small, he will be exceedingly liberal and generous. He will find it difficult to withstand the solicitations of charity, and will be especially alive to the interests of his friends. With Acquisitiveness large, he will be well disposed to charitable objects, but will seldom ever give to them substantial aid. He will be more likely to give his time and advice than money. If, with this combination large, Love of Approbation be added, it will greatly aid the effect of Benevolence. With but moderate Destructiveness, it will be difficult for him to witness suffering or pain; yet, with large Destructiveness, when it is necessary, notwithstanding his general kindness of disposition, can witness and even inflict pain, and take pleasure in it.

MODERATE.—With Benevolence moderate, one will be kindly and well disposed towards others, yet, except on extraordinary occasions, will not make many sacrifices to their good. If Acquisitiveness and the Selfish Feelings generally are large, he will be avaricious and selfish to the last degree, and yet not be absolutely insensible to the claims of the unfortunate. If Love of Approbation is large, he may often give to charitable purposes, but it will be more for the sake of having his acts the subject of conversation than out of good will to the object. If Self-esteem, Combativeness and Destructiveness are large, he will be harsh, cruel and severe, and will be apparently utterly regardless of the feelings of his fellow men.

SMALL.—With Benevolence but small, one will be unfeeling and cruel. If Conscientiousness is large, he will not trespass on the rights of others in any particular, but his whole conduct will exhibit, notwithstanding, a disregard of all the tender amenities of life, and an almost utter absence of sympathy and good feeling.

4. HOPE.

THIS organ induces the mind to contemplate the future with high anticipations of being able to realize whatever the other feelings desire. It thus causes us to be gay and cheerful, and to preserve the equanimity of our temper amidst difficulties and misfortune. Those who are destitute of it are prone to disobedience. Their ideas of the future are always dark and gloomy.

PREDOMINANT.—With Hope predominant, an individual is constantly revelling in the bright prospects of the future. He will be so sanguine of success, that he will neglect the means by which success can be attained. He will be credulous and visionary in all his enterprises and undertakings.

LARGE.—With Hope large, one always views the future with bright anticipations. If Caution and Causality are large, he will never be carried away by his expectations, but will pursue generally a prudent course, and not allow his hopes to hurry him into imprudent measures. If Combativeness, Firmness, Self-esteem and Ideality are large, he will be bold, speculative and enterprising; and if Caution is small, will be excessively rash, precipitate and imprudent, often attempting undertakings which to the less sanguine appear impossible. With this combination, he will never be cast down or discouraged; the vicissitudes of fortune have no power to repress his energy or restrain his enterprise.

MODERATE.—With Hope moderate, one's expectations will be sanguine, but not immoderately so. If Firmness, Self-esteem, Combativeness and Destructiveness are large, he will attempt important undertakings, and count with much certainty and pleasure their chances of success. If Cautiousness is large, he will despond much more than hope, will never attempt enterprises, unless their chances of success are almost certain; will expect too little, rather than too much, and will not be sanguine or cheerful.

SMALL.—With Hope small, a person will be constantly low spirited and melancholy. The brightest prospects can hardly excite his spirits. He will dwell perpetually upon the dark side of appearances, and will want enterprise and spirit.

5. MARVELLOUSNESS.

THIS organ produces credulity of mind. It predisposes to believe without sufficient testimony, and delights in contemplating the strange and wonderful. It has been supposed, that this organ is given to enable the mind to believe in those passages in Revelation, in which supernatural performances are related, and that consequently it increases the zeal and fervour of the devout and religious. Its more general manifestations, are to give a fondness for supernatural stories, and a love of the strange, the new and the marvellous, and sometimes leads to a desire to visit mysterious and unfrequented countries.

PREDOMINANT.—With Marvellousness predominant, one will be exceedingly credulous and visionary in all his views. He will readily take for granted whatever is told him of a wonderful character. He will disregard simple causes, and be disposed to account for any thing a little unusual by a forced and unnatural conclusion.

LARGE.—With Marvellousness large, and Veneration large, a person, if religious, will be eminently devout and superstitious. He will readily believe in special providences, divine agency, &c. With large Eventuality and Ideality, will be passionately fond of reading marvellous accounts, hair-breadth escapes, &c. With large Cautiousness, and small Causality, will be afraid of ghosts, and will profess often to see apparitions.

MODERATE.—With but a moderate developement of this organ, and with large Causality and Comparison, one will be rather sceptical in his views, requiring much proof before his assent can be gained, yet at the same time, will keep his mind open to conviction, and will be willing to give subjects a considerate examination. If Causality is small, he will often adopt principles upon insufficient grounds; and with Ideality large, will be exceedingly fond of marvellous tales, and of fictitious excitement of a mysterious character.

SMALL.—With Marvellousness small, one will be exceedingly incredulous and sceptical. It will be impossible for him to believe any thing but what is susceptible of the clearest demonstration. With Ideality moderate or small, he will have great aversion to marvellous stories and fictitious works generally. With Veneration small, he may be religious, but his mind will be peculiar. He will not submit to the teaching of any man, and will form his creed from the results of his own reading and reflection.

INTELLECTUAL SENTIMENTS.

1. IDEALITY.

THIS organ imparts a relish and a desire for the beautiful, the elevated and the exquisite. It renders its possessor constantly alive to impressions of beauty, and leads to a desire of improvement. Those who possess it large are never satisfied with sober reality; but delight to revel in the illusions of fancied existence.

PREDOMINANT.—With Ideality predominant, one will live in a state of constant illusion. He will be enthusiastic and chimerical in all his views and opinions. His enjoyments will be of the most intense description, and his suffering of the same character. Plain matter of fact and sober reality will disgust him. He will be ever striving after the refined and the ideal. He will be an enthusiastic admirer of poetry and the fine arts, and all objects of taste.

LARGE.—With this organ large, one will possess a rich and glowing fancy, and a natural refinement and exquisiteness of taste. With Benevolence large, he will be much afflicted at the miseries of mankind, and will long for a state of existence where happiness is unalloyed and pleasure interminable. With Adhesiveness large, his ideas of friendship will be of the most exquisite and refined description. With Colour, Form and Size large, he will be an excellent judge of paintings, and will be exceedingly fond of them; with Locality and Form large, will take great delight in picturesque scenery, in flowers, trees, &c. With large Language and Comparison, will employ many metaphors and figures of speech in his writings and conversations; with Self-esteem and Comparison large, he will be exceedingly choice in his use of language; and if, with this combination, Language be large, and Causality small, he will have many more words than ideas, and will converse much more than think. He will be superficial and showy, rather than solid. With Amativeness and Adhesiveness large, will be fond of such poetry as is the subject of love and passion. With Imitation and Marvellousness large, will never relapse in his efforts for improvement.

MODERATE.—With Ideality moderate, one will not be insensible to the beauties of nature and art, yet will never allow his fancy to obtain the mastery over him. He will seldom experience a high degree of enthusiasm and rapture of feeling, and be rather a plain and matter-of-fact character. If Causality is large, he may relish fiction, but it will be more for its sentiment than for its ideal qualities. If Self-esteem is small, his language will be exceedingly plain, and he will never attain a high degree of refinement and polish of manners.

SMALL.—With Ideality small, one will be incapable of appreciating beauty. His views and sentiments will be coarse and unrefined. His expressions will be low and vulgar. He will have great aversion to poetry, paintings and all works of taste.

2. CONSTRUCTIVENESS.

THIS organ furnishes the inclination to construct, to build, and to invent. It is supposed by many, that this organ of itself is a proof of the ability to be an operative mechanic, but this is an error; the office of the organ is only to manifest the desire by which the intellect is excited to its gratification. To possess a high degree of inventive power, one must not only possess a large organ of Constructiveness, but a favourable intellect; and to be a successful practical mechanic, it is requisite to have along with these two requisites, a large developement of Form, Size, Weight, &c.

PREDOMINANT.—With Constructiveness predominant, one will possess a high degree of natural ability for planning, contriving, building, &c. He will take great delight in contemplating works of architecture, and other subjects of human ingenuity.

LARGE.—With large Constructiveness and Imitation, one will excel in making after a pattern; but if Form, Size and Weight are small, he will be unable to construct from his own invention.

3. IMITATION.

THE function of this organ is to enable its possessor to do whatever he has witnessed performed by others. It leads to a desire to represent, mimic, act, copy, &c. It greatly facilitates the learning of a foreign language, and is an essential ingredient in the character of the skilful mechanic. The gestures of the active are prompted by the same feeling.

PREDOMINANT.—With this organ predominant will be given to practice mimicry and representation. If Secretiveness is large, he will be well calculated for the stage, and can readily represent any feeling or sentiment that he may be enabled to conceive. With large Eventuality, Individuality and Mirthfulness, will readily notice all the peculiarities of his associates, and be perpetually turning them into ridicule.

LARGE.—With large Love of Approbation, Ideality, Self-esteem, Individuality and Secretiveness, one will be able readily to adapt himself to the customs and forms of any society in which he may be thrown. With this combination and tolerably favourable opportunities for observation, his manners will be highly polished and agreeable. With large Form, Size and

Ideality, can readily copy or imitate a superscription, or other writing, and with proper discipline will excel in drawing. With large Constructiveness, Form and Size, will be highly capable of excelling in a mechanical profession. With large Secretiveness, can relate stories with great force. With large Secretiveness, Individuality, Eventuality, Language and Comparison, he will excel in description, and be capable of giving force and life to his ideas that will fasten them upon the recollection of his auditors. With Secretiveness and Firmness large, can restrain the expression of pain in the most heroic manner, and assume the appearance of perfect health. If Secretiveness is small, he will be unable to imitate a character, or mimic, yet will nevertheless be able to draw, &c.

MODERATE.—With but a moderate developement of this organ, one will find great difficulty in description, imitating, or in any performance that requires the exercise of this faculty. With large Secretiveness, he will be enabled to relate stories, but he can never be able to represent any continued action, or carry out a successful description.

SMALL.—With Imitation small, an individual will be almost wholly destitute of the attributes ascribed to this organ. He will be unable to represent very accurately the simplest actions. Can never excel in penmanship or drawing, and will always be distinguished as an original. If Self-esteem is large, he will dispel ceremony; if Secretiveness is small, he will be perfectly unique in his actions, and be distinguished for his independence and eccentricity.

4. MIRTHFULNESS.

THIS organ gives the desire and the ability to enjoy mirth. Its possessors are apt to consider things in their most humorous light, to the neglect of their more sober characteristics. It is that principle of the mind, which enables one to detect what is absurd and ridiculous, and to delight in jokes, fun and laughter.

PREDOMINANT.—With Mirthfulness predominant, one has an irresistible tendency to view every thing in a comical aspect. His most serious meditations are liable to be interrupted by mirthful intrusions; and he will indulge his humorous propensities, regardless of consequences.

LARGE.—With Mirthfulness large, will have a lively perception of the ludicrous, and will be apt to catch up every little incident, and make it the subject of humorous remarks. With Destructiveness and Comparison large, he will be sarcastic, and severe in his jokes, and will laugh heartily at the discomfiture of others. If Secretiveness and Imitation are small, he will not be able to relate a joke with propriety, yet will enjoy one; but if Secretiveness, Ideality and Imitation are large, he will tell a story in the most refined and delightful manner; with Comparison and Love of Approbation large, and Causality and Secretiveness moderate, he will laugh excessively at his own jokes.

MODERATE.—With Mirthfulness moderate, one is fond of fun, but unable to make it. With Combativeness, Destructiveness and Comparison large, will be severe and pungent in his attempts at wit, and will thus often give offence.

SMALL.—With Mirthfulness but small, one will be nearly destitute of the ability to enjoy a joke, and quite unable to make one. He will look upon wit as impertinent and silly, and be offended at jocose remarks. If Love of Approbation is large, he will be very much annoyed at jokes; with Combativeness moderate or large, will get highly offended at any attempts to do so.

OBSERVING FACULTIES.

1. INDIVIDUALITY.

THE function of this organ is to recognise existences, or the identity of substances without reference to their peculiarities; it has been termed the memory of things. Its recollective powers are limited to simple details, or facts having no reference to their form, colour, &c.

PREDOMINANT.—One in whom Individuality is predominant, will be distinguished for his powers of observation. No object will escape his scrutiny, and no opportunities will satiate his curiosity. If his reflective powers are weak, he will require a great mass of facts, but they will lie in his mind confused and unoccupied: he will be unable to employ them in illustration or argument. If in the habit of writing, his compositions will abound with personifications. If Causality is large, and Concentrativeness is small, his reflective powers will be weakened by the tendency imparted by individuality to dwell upon substances instead of causes.

LARGE.—With Individuality large, one is induced to observe and examine every object that comes under the limits of his vision. His scrutiny does not appear to include the peculiarities of substances, but rests satisfied with their mere corporeal existence. He is distinguished as a close observer of men and things. In description he is exceedingly minute; and with Concentrativeness large, prolix and tedious to the last degree. With Eventuality and Time large, he will not only notice quickly, but will remember with exactness; and with Language large, can describe accurately events, manners, customs, &c. With these organs large, he will have a great desire for reading, and for collecting facts. With the Reflective Powers and Language large, will be much given to reflection, and in expressing his thoughts will be clear and perspicuous.

MODERATE.—With Individuality moderate, and the Reflective Powers and Concentrativeness large, will be subject to abstraction of mind, and will be much more given to reflection than to observation, still, when any thing peculiar is offered to his attention, he can readily examine its character. He will generally notice existences more in relation to their uses and adaptations, than as mere identities.

SMALL.—A person whose Individuality is small, is generally heedless and unobserving. With Locality moderate or small, he may travel extensively; and yet remain as ignorant as if he had staid at home. Nothing but the more obvious characteristics has power to excite his attention. If

Constructiveness and Ideality are full, he will notice works of architecture, but his descriptions of such will lack unity in consequence of his incapacity to notice details. If Causality and Comparison are large, he will be addicted to reflection, but his expressions will be vague and apparently inconsistent, consequent on his inability to collect minute details.

2. FORM.

THIS organ gives the ability to discriminate forms. It aids the artist, and a prominent developement is indispensable to the skilful mechanic.

PREDOMINANT.—With Form predominant, one never forgets the appearance of any thing that has once came distinctly under his cognition. He will readily discriminate the forms of objects at a distance, and perceive differences and resemblances where many others will not; can recollect the name of a person by remembering its appearance when written; will easily detect typographical errors; and with Size and Individuality large, can read with great facility and correctness.

LARGE.—With Form large, one much more readily recollects the appearance of a person than his name, this is more particularly the case with Individuality large. With Individuality small, he will not be apt to pay attention to ordinary matters, but if his attention is called to them, he recollects their appearance with distinctness. With Imitation large, he will be able to draw and copy with great facility, and will excel in penmanship.

MODERATE.—With Form moderate, and the Reflecting organs large, one will never notice the shapes of substances, until something particular enforces his attention. He will then require considerable examination to enable him to recognise them afterwards. His recollection of persons and things will usually be confused and indistinct. With Individuality large, observes much, and with tolerable distinctness; but with Individuality small, is heedless and inattentive.

SMALL.—With Form small, a person will be unable to recollect the countenances of persons even with whom he is intimate. He will be apt to miscall words in reading. He will find it difficult to decipher obscure handwriting. It will also be difficult, if not impossible, for him to make much progress in the natural sciences.

3. SIZE.

THIS organ gives the idea of space, and the power of judging the relative dimensions of objects; it also gives the ability to judge of distances or of lineal space.

PREDOMINANT.—With Size predominant, one's perceptions of the dimensions of objects will be singularly accurate, he will be enabled to tell at a mere glance the dimensions of a room, the length and relative distances of objects, the centre of a circle, and to perform any other action requiring the exercise of this organ.

LARGE.—With Size large, one will possess all the attributes ascribed to Size predominant, but in a minor degree.

MODERATE.—With Size but moderate, and without having been accustomed to the exercise of the organ, one will greatly err in judging of the dimensions of objects and size generally.

SMALL.—With Size small, one will be signally deficient in all the qualities ascribed to this organ.

4. WEIGHT.

THE office of this organ is to impart to its possessor the idea of the power of gravity, or of mechanical force and resistance. It gives great ability to judge of momentum, and is large in the heads of all those who excel in fencing, boxing, archery, skating, quoit playing, &c.

PREDOMINANT.—With Weight predominant, one will be remarkable for his power in the use of this faculty. In performing gymnastic feats, in balancing, riding a fractious horse, and in every other exercise that requires a display of agility he will be pre-eminently conspicuous.

LARGE.—With Weight and Self-esteem large, one can easily adapt himself to the laws of gravity, will never fall in precarious situations, can go aloft at sea in the most intrepid manner, and readily perform any operation requiring the exercise of this endowment.

MODERATE.—With Weight but moderate, one will be rather deficient in the qualities ascribed to the functions of this organ, but with practice, may attain considerable skill and success in the arts to which it conduces.

SMALL.—With Weight but small, one will easily lose his balance, even in situations where no danger is to be apprehended. He will be enabled to excel as a marksman or wrestler; will be enabled to learn to skate, or to pitch quoits. With large Form, Constructiveness and Imitation, will have a mechanical turn, but will be unable to excel as a machinist in consequence of his inability to perform the functions ascribed to this organ.

5. COLOUR.

THIS organ gives the perception of Colour, and renders one sensible to their different shades, their harmony and discord.

PREDOMINANT.—With this organ predominant, one will notice the colour of an object before any other peculiarity appertaining to it; will take delight in colours, in their arrangement, order and beauty.

LARGE.—With Colour, Ideality and Comparison large, one will be distinguished for his love of colours, and his ability to discriminate and arrange them. With large Form, Ideality, Individuality, Constructiveness and Imitation, Size and Order, will excel as a portrait painter, and take great delight in that occupation; and with Eventuality, Locality and Comparison, as an historical painter.

MODERATE.—With Colour but moderate, and in an occupation that does not exercise the function of this organ, one will be decidedly deficient in his ability to discriminate colours, but if his pursuits are the reverse of what is here presumed, he will be a tolerable judge of colours, and possess considerable taste in his arrangement and selection of them.

SMALL.—With this organ but small, an individual will be unable to discriminate any but the most striking colours. With Ideality large, may be fond of paintings, but will be unable to point out their peculiar beauties. He can never tell the colour of the eyes or hair of even his familiar acquaintances.

6. ORDER.

THIS organ imparts that quality of mind, which prompts an individual to preserve order and arrangement in his several pursuits and occupations. The peculiar action of the organ is much dependent upon the character of the other developements.

PREDOMINANT.—With this organ predominant, one will be distinguished for his love of order and arrangement. His maxim will be "*a place for every thing, and every thing in its place.*" This quality of mind will be a prominent trait in his character, and will influence to a great degree his conduct and actions.

LARGE.—With this organ large, one will be much annoyed by disorder; his room, clothes, books, papers, and every thing under his control, will always be kept in the utmost neatness and regularity. With Adhesiveness large, will be fond of social enjoyments, but his pleasures will be much interrupted on discovering a want of neatness and order in the persons of his friends and acquaintances. With Ideality and Individuality large, will be exceedingly neat and fastidious. With Combativeness and Destructiveness large, will easily get offended and angry at seeing things out of place. With Locality large, he will be enabled to perform actions in places in the dark, with which he is acquainted almost as well as in the light. With Ideality but moderate or small, he will be slovenly in his dress and appearance, yet preserve order, arrangement and neatness with his books, papers, &c.

MODERATE.—With Order but moderate, one will be rather deficient in the qualities ascribed to this organ. He will be fond of order, and acknowledge its utility, but will be unable to observe it. With Ideality large, and having been educated in habits of order and neatness, the action of this organ will be much improved. He will possess most of the qualities ascribed to Order large, but will never sacrifice much to this quality of mind; but with Ideality small, and with an imperfect education, he will be slovenly, loose and irregular in all his actions and movements.

SMALL.—With this organ small, one will be exceedingly disorderly and incoherent in all his arrangements, and business details. His actions will not be guided by system, his books, papers, &c. will be left where he happens to use them. He will be unable to appreciate the utility of order, and complain of those who practice it as being over nice.

7. CALCULATION.

THIS organ enables us to form the idea of number, or the plurality of objects. It assists in the recollection of dates and quantities. It enables one to readily understand numbers and their combinations. Its activity takes place, whenever there is a departure from unity. A large endowment of this organ is not essential to the algebraist and geometrician, its functions being limited to arithmetical calculations.

PREDOMINANT.—One having Calculation predominant, will reckon in his head almost any arithmetical problem that can be proposed to him. If Causality and Comparison are large, he will excel in the higher branches of mathematics, and possess a great fondness for these studies.

LARGE.—With calculation large, one will be distinguished among his acquaintances for his skill in arithmetical calculations. He will be enabled to tell at a glance, operations which to an ordinary accountant require the use of figures. If Causality and Comparison are large, he will excel in solving difficult problems in the higher mathematics, but if these organs are deficient, his talent will be limited to arithmetical calculations.

MODERATE.—With Calculation moderate, and in a situation which constantly demands the act of ready calculation, one may become highly talented in this respect. He will, however, require time and effort to go through an intricate operation. If Causality and Comparison are large, in ordinary circumstances he will accustom himself to the use of a slate and pencil for all operations of a complicated character.

SMALL.—With Calculation small, one can succeed in arithmetical calculations only by dint of great labour, and then only to a limited extent. If Causality and Comparison are large, he may be capable of the higher branches of mathematics, but the difficulty, which his arithmetical calculations cost him, will render him averse to all mathematical speculations.

8. LOCALITY.

THIS organ gives the power of noticing and recollecting the peculiar position of objects, and gives a desire for travelling, and for the study of geography. It is essential to the scene painter. It strongly aids the power of association.

PREDOMINANT.—With Locality predominant, one will have an insatiable desire for travelling, roving about, and for visiting strange places, will readily recollect their peculiar position, the localities of the prominent objects of attention, and will be excessively fond of reading geography and works of travels.

LARGE.—With Locality large, one will have a great desire for travelling; and with Acquisitiveness and Inhabitiveness moderate or small, will be prompted to roam about regardless of expense, or of family considerations. In visiting strange places, he readily notices their peculiar localities, and will ever after recollect them. He will be excessively fond of studying geography, and works of travels; and will be enabled to point out the particular position of a sentence in a book or newspaper containing an idea to which he wishes to direct attention. He will never stumble in the dark, and will find his way with little instruction through unfrequented places.

MODERATE.—With Locality but moderate, one will have but little desire for travelling, and will be nearly regardless of the localities of the places which he visits. He will often lose his way in forests and cities, with which he is not familiar, and will seldom find a place if obscurely situated without great trouble. With Individuality and Ideality large, will have a fine taste for natural scenery, but his descriptions will be vague and unsatisfactory in consequence of his inability to point out the particular localities of the different objects.

SMALL.—With Locality small, one will be extremely unobservant of, and inattentive to the localities of objects. He will often lose his way even in places with which he is familiar, and will be nearly wanting in the attributes ascribed to this organ.

9. EVENTUALITY.

THIS organ takes cognizance of actions as they exist; and thus observes the phenomena that is constantly taking place throughout nature. It is a principal element in the desire for knowledge, and greatly aids in giving an ability for practical business involving details.

PREDOMINANT.—With Eventuality predominant, one will notice and remember every transaction and occurrence that comes within his observation, in all their varied details. He will have an insatiable thirst for knowledge, and seldom allow any incident to escape his recollection. He will attend much more to facts than to principles, and will be given more to narration than to reasoning, often weakening his arguments by narrating unimportant particulars, which have little connexion with the point contested.

LARGE.—Those in whom this organ is large, possess a clear and distinct recollection of events and transactions, and are much given to reading and observation. They are particularly fond of historical and other works, abounding in facts and incidents. With Language large, will be fond of relating with extreme minuteness, occurrences and facts with which he is familiar. If Concentrativeness is large his narrations will be given in a clear and connected style; but if Concentrativeness is small, they will want method and connexion. With large Individuality, Language and Comparison, he will possess a great thirst for knowledge, and will readily collect, analyze and classify ideas. If, with this combination, Causality being moderate or small, he will have a large fund of knowledge, but be unable to profit by it.

MODERATE.—With Eventuality moderate, one will be able usually to observe actions, but will be inattentive to any but those of the most striking character. If Causality and Comparison are large, will possess a ready power of reasoning and classification, but will be wanting in facts and details to sustain his own opinions. He will be more given to reason than narration, and will collect facts more for the purpose of illustrating his arguments, than the pleasure of acquiring them.

SMALL.—With Eventuality small, one will be decidedly deficient in his recollection of facts and incidents, and will be dull and incurious. He will be enabled to follow any occupation requiring a close attention to details. In narrating, he will be unable to recollect any but the most striking points.

10. TIME.

THIS organ gives the ability to observe and recollect the lapses of time. It also confers the power of keeping time in music and dancing.

PREDOMINANT.—With Time predominant, one will possess an astonishing facility in recollecting dates, the ages of individuals, time at which occurrences have taken place, and the lapses of time generally.

LARGE.—With Time large, one will readily recollect the date of transactions that have come under his attention, will be fond of history, and will especially recollect the precise time of each event. He will be enabled to perform an action at the given word of command. If in the habit of dancing, will excel, and take great delight in that amusement. He will be able to judge the hour of the day, without the aid of a time piece, with accuracy.

MODERATE.—With Time moderate, one will recollect none but the most important dates. If Eventuality is large, will be fond of history, but will generally forget the time of transactions, and thus want clearness in his historical knowledge. He will often forget the day of the week and even his own age.

SMALL.—With this organ small, one will be nearly deficient in the attributes ascribed to its functions.

11. TUNE.

THIS organ gives the taste for music, and makes its possessor take a high degree of pleasure in listening to musical performances.

PREDOMINANT.—With this organ predominant, one will have an exquisite taste for music, will make any sacrifices to enjoy the pleasure it imparts, and will readily catch and learn tunes almost by intuition.

LARGE.—With this organ large, one will have a superior taste for music, and will easily learn tunes, and if his voice be good, will easily learn to sing. If Ideality is large, his performances will be rich and pathetic.

MODERATE.—With this organ moderate, one will possess a considerable taste for music, and with a good voice and large Imitation, may learn to sing from hearing others, but can never excel.

SMALL.—With this organ small, one may be fond of music of particular kinds to which he has been accustomed, but this will not enable him to learn or practice music.

12. LANGUAGE.

THE function of this organ is to enable its possessor to express his ideas in appropriate language, and thus to communicate thoughts and sentiments. The talent of verbal memory depends on this organ.

PREDOMINANT.—Those in whom this organ predominates abound with words. They talk merely for the sake of talking, and their style in writing and speaking is characterized by great verbosity. In ordinary conversation they will use a great multitude of words to express a common idea, and will be distinguished among their acquaintance as intolerable talkers. They will be able to commit words to memory with readiness, and will recollect forms of expression, where otherwise the idea would escape them.

LARGE.—With Language large, one will possess the qualities to a great extent that are ascribed to Language predominant. With large Individuality, Form, Locality and Eventuality, will be enabled to relate with great accuracy the conversation of a speaker, his looks, tones and actions, and will readily recall the precise words used. He will possess great ability to acquire knowledge, and will be distinguished for copiousness, ease and volubility of expression. If Causality and Comparison are moderate or small, his ideas will be of a crude, imperfect character, yet he will converse incessantly nevertheless. With Comparison large, his knowledge of language will be superior, but if Comparison is small his words will often be incorrect and applied in a wrong sense.

MODERATE.—With Language but moderate on ordinary occasions, one will be wanting in powers of expression, and to express his ideas with fluency and effect, he will require much excitement. If Causality and Comparison are large, with a large and active brain, he will have many important ideas, but they will lose much of their cogency for want of more appropriate expressions. With Secretiveness large, he will be rather taciturn and indisposed for conversation.

SMALL.—With Language small, one will be unable to express any but the most common ideas without hesitation and embarrassment. He will find it difficult and almost impossible to commit to memory, and his style of speaking and writing will be dry and common place; talking will be to him a burthen.

REFLECTIVE FACULTIES.

1. CAUSALITY.

THIS organ observes the relation of cause and effect, and discriminates between actions and the causes which produce them. It enables an individual to adopt the requisite means to effect any end. It is the active element in every effort of reflection, and is the grand source of thought and originality of mind.

PREDOMINANT.—With Causality predominant, an individual will be distinguished for his proneness to thought, and utility to speculate and discuss abstractions. Whatever subject is suggested, or point discussed, he will be liable to enquire for reasons and causes. He will be given much more to reflection than observation.

LARGE.—With Causality large, one will be enabled readily to perceive the relation between an effect and the cause which produced it. He will be distinguished for gravity and thoughtfulness of mind; and will possess much sagacity, penetration, and originality. With Conscientiousness, Veneration and Marvellousness large, and the selfish propensities moderate or small, he will be much given to moral investigations, and to reading and conversing upon subjects connected with general utility and public morals. With Combativeness large, he will be inclined to argument and disputation. With the Perceptive organs but moderate, he will pay more attention to principles than facts, and will be guided more by reason and experience.

MODERATE.—With Causality moderate, and with proper culture, one may possess good judgment and a reasoning turn of mind, but he will be destitute of originality and force of thought. In an occupation or course of life to which he has been accustomed, he will conduct with prudence and propriety, but will be deficient in the necessary power to devise means for extraordinary operations, lay new plans, and to carry into effect important operations. With large Individuality, Imitation and Love of Approbation, and small Self-esteem, he will be destitute of any marked characteristics of his own, and will readily adapt himself to the views and opinions of his companions.

SMALL.—With Causality small, one will be utterly deficient in originality and force of mind, and will be wanting in that quality of character which renders men calm, judicious, penetrating and discerning. With the propensities and sentiments properly balanced, he will possess discretion, and be enabled to conduct operations to which he has been accustomed.

2. COMPARISON.

THE office of this organ is to enable us to compare differences, to note resemblances, and to perceive analogies. By it we are enabled to adapt one thing to another so as to produce a harmonious whole. It prompts to the use of figurative language in writing and conversation. Those in whom it is large, trace similitudes and affinities between objects and events which entirely escape the observation of others in whom the organ is small. It prompts to reasoning, but not in the line of necessary consequence. It explains one thing by comparing it with another. It gives ingenuity in discovering unexpected glimpses and superficial coincidences.

PREDOMINANT.—With Comparison predominant, one will be enabled to analyze subjects, and to detect inconsistencies with the greatest facility and readiness, and will almost intuitively perceive the misapplication of facts and principles. His expressions will be characterized by great precision and clearness, and his arguments will be explained with a great variety of happy illustrations.

LARGE.—With Comparison large, one will be strongly given to criticising and analyzing, and will readily detect fallacies and improprieties that would escape the observation of those in whom this organ is small. If Ideality and Individuality are large, his language will abound with elevated metaphors and figures of speech, but if Causality is small, his judgment will be defective. If Secretiveness is small, and Combativeness and Self-esteem large, he will be strongly inclined to criticise every observation he hears, and will thus excite enmity and ill-will. With large Eventuality and Individuality, will have a great taste for the study of natural science, and will be extremely fond of classifying their phenomena, and of comparing the various qualities of physical objects with each. He will likewise be fond of the study of history, and will habitually compare and classify the various transactions with those of similar characteristics. If the Perceptive organs generally are large and Causality small, he will be possessed of good practical talents, but will be devoid of originality of mind. He will be calculated to succeed in a course of life in which he has the example of able men, but he will be utterly unable to deviate from the beaten road and assume the lead for himself.

MODERATE.—With Comparison but moderate, one's powers of analyzation and criticism will not be conspicuous. With an active brain and a favourable intellect generally, he will be enabled to perceive the force of figurative language, and will often indulge in it, but his metaphors will lack force and appropriateness. With Individuality and Eventuality large, will possess a great store of facts, but will be unable to arrange and classify them. If Causality is large, he will readily perceive the errors in an argument, but he will lack the power to point out and apply the exact replication.

SMALL.—One having Comparison small, will be excessively dull, and will lack discernment and discrimination. The most obvious resemblances can hardly be made manifest to him.

TEMPERAMENTS.

THE term Temperament, says a late writer, is applied to those differences of external appearance which are supposed to indicate the comparative state of the fibres of the body as they are more or less dense, or as possessing one of the functions of life in greater activity, or one of the constituents of the animal body in greater quantity than another; or in short, certain states or conditions of the body, which are found to exercise more or less influence in exciting or repressing the action of the organs.

The Temperaments as they are usually enumerated, are four in number, to wit: the Lymphatic; the Sanguine; the Bilious; and the Nervous.

In persons of a Lymphatic Temperament, the brain is sluggish and performs its functions in a feeble but steady manner. The individual is averse to severe exertion, and requires much stimuli to move him. As a general rule, he will be averse to either mental or bodily activity.

Those of a Sanguine Temperament are easily excited, and easily depressed, fond of pleasure, and averse to severe exertions. They live for the present, rather than the future. The actions of the mind are quick, rather than powerful.

Persons of a Bilious Temperament are determined, persevering and ambitious in their character and disposition. Their every movement and aspect indicates decision of purpose. Their mental operations are vigorous and powerful.

Persons of a Nervous Temperament, are very sensitive, and are easily excited. Their mental operations are rapid, but they are soon exhausted.

THE END.

Milton Keynes UK
Ingram Content Group UK Ltd.
UKHW012315040624
443649UK00007B/652